THE SMALLEST

FASCINATING FACTS

David Armentrout

he Rourke Press, Inc.
Beach, Florida 32964

PHOTO CREDITS
© Armentrout: Title page; © Denso Corporation: Right Cover, pg.
4; © Kim Karpeles: pg 10; © A. L. Katres: pg. 8; © Ron
McPherson: pg. 13; © Orion/Int'l Stock: pg. 12; © James P.
Rowan: Left Cover, pgs. 7, 17; © Lynn M. Stone: pg. 15; © Doris
VanBuskirk: pg. 18; © Oscar C. Williams: pg. 21

Library of Congress Cataloging-in-Publication Data

Armentrout, David, 1962–
      The smallest / by David Armentrout.
         p. cm. — (Fascinating facts)
      ISBN 1-57103-130-8
      Summary: Brief presentations of facts about some of the
smallest things in the world.
      1. Size perception—Juvenile literature. [1. Size.]
I. Title II. Series: Armentrout, David, 1962-   Fascinating facts.
BF299.S5A77 1996
031.02—dc20   96–20858
                                                                                      CIP
                                                                                      AC

Printed in the USA

TABLE OF CONTENTS

CAR

What looks like a car, runs like a car, but can't be driven like a car? It is the world's smallest motorized car. The microcar is as tiny as one grain of rice!

The microcar is made up of 24 parts. It has wheels, head lights, tail lights, front and rear bumpers, and even a spare tire.

At first the car could only be moved by a magnet under a table. Designers then installed a real working motor made up of five parts.

The microcar, shown here on a penny, is no bigger than a grain of rice

BIRD

Hummingbirds are the smallest of all birds. The bee hummingbird is the tiniest: It weighs much less than an ounce and is only two inches long.

Most hummingbirds live in tropical areas. They eat the nectar of flowers, using their long bills to collect pollen.

Hummingbirds get their name from the soft hum their wings make as they fly. Hummingbirds hover in one place as their wings beat as fast as 80 times per second. Did you know that hummingbirds can fly backwards?

A hummingbird uses its long bill to gather nectar from flowers

COUNTRY

Vatican City, the smallest country in the world, is in Rome. The Vatican is home to the government of the Roman Catholic Church, called the Holy See.

Two of Vatican City's most fascinating buildings are Saint Peter's **Basilica** (buh SIL i kuh), the largest Catholic church, and the Sistine Chapel.

Michelangelo, famous for his 16th Century art, painted the ceiling of the Sistine Chapel while lying on his back on a scaffold. It took him four years to do the paintings.

Millions of people visit Saint Peter's Basilica yearly to see the historical works of art

PLANT

Some people are experts at growing tiny trees and plants. **Bonsai** (bone SY) is the ancient Japanese art of growing and shaping small trees and plants.

Almost any woody plant can be grown as bonsai. The plants are put in small containers and given plenty of sunshine, water, fertilizer, and special care.

Expert growers carefully prune, trim, and shape the plants into miniature forms of the normal-sized plant.

Bonsai trees are miniatures of
regular size trees

Chihuahuas have large upright ears

"Arbet," the world's smallest street-legal car, has 5,000 hand-made parts

BONE AND MUSCLE

The ear is an organ of the body made up of three parts: the outer, middle, and inner ear. The middle ear contains the smallest bone and muscle in the body.

The **stapes** (STAY peez), the smallest bone, sends vibrations from the eardrum to the inner ear. The **stapedius** (sta PEE dee us), the smallest muscle, controls the movement of the stapes.

Our sense of hearing would not be possible without these two tiny, yet important, parts of the body.

This model shows the inside of a human ear

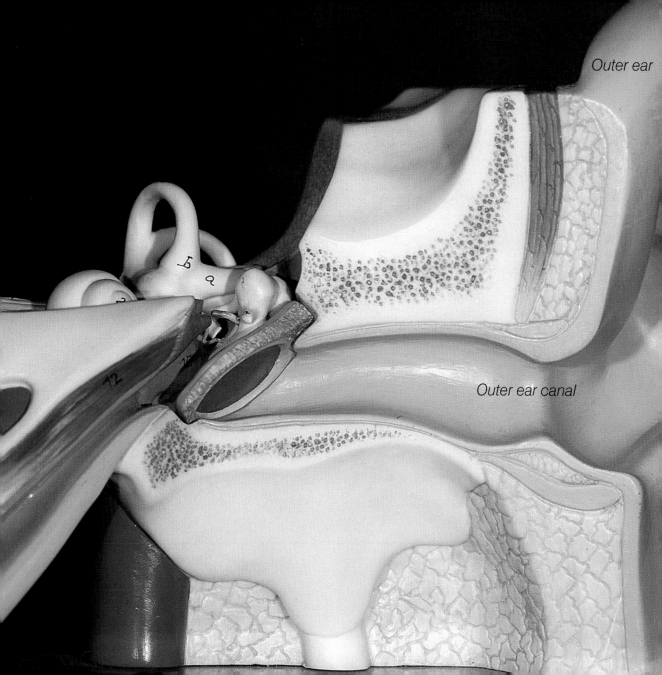

Outer ear

Outer ear canal

PONY

A pony is a small breed, or kind, of horse. The Shetland is the smallest breed of pony. Shetlands usually do not stand taller than 40 inches at the shoulder.

The Shetland, native to the Shetland Islands of Scotland, is a sturdy animal. Two visible traits are strong legs and a thick mane.

Children like to ride Shetland ponies because of their gentle nature and small size. They are often seen giving rides to children at county and state fairs.

The Shetland pony is the smallest breed of pony

MAMMAL

Shrews are the smallest of all mammals. They look like mice, with long pointed snouts and tiny ears and eyes. The pygmy shrew is about two-and-a-half-inches long, including its tail.

Shrews have high **metabolism** (mi TAB uh LIZ um). This means their food digests very quickly. To live, shrews need to eat about 70 percent of their body weight in food each day. That isn't much food, though, since the pygmy shrew weighs less than an ounce.

The shrew is a nocturnal mammal,
which means it is active at night

DOG

Dogs come in all shapes, sizes, and colors. The smallest breeds are called toys. The smallest toy breed is the **Chihuahua** (chi WAH wah), named after a part of Mexico.

Some Chihuahuas have long hair, others have short hair. Their coats may be white or black or a combination of colors. Chihuahua dogs have large upright ears and a fairly long tail.

Chihuahuas can weigh up to 8 pounds or as little as 1 pound. They usually stand about 5 inches at the shoulder.

The smallest toy breed is the Chihuahua

STATE

Rhode Island, the smallest state, is in the northeastern United States. If traveling across the state, you would need to travel only 47 miles from north to south, or 40 miles from east to west.

Rhode Island is big in history, though. One of the original thirteen colonies, Rhode Island was the first colony to declare freedom from Great Britain.

People enjoy swimming, fishing, and boating in Rhode Island's coastal waters. The "America's Cup" yachting race drew many people to Newport, Rhode Island, from 1930 to 1983.

Glossary

basilica (buh SIL i kuh) — an early Christian church

bonsai (bone SY) — a plant or tree grown small by special methods; the art of growing small versions of normal-sized plants

Chihuahua (chi WAH wah) — a very small dog (about five inches high)

metabolism (mi TAB uh LIZ um) — the processes of the body breaking down food

stapedius (sta PEE dee us) — a small muscle in the ear that controls the movement of the smallest bone (stapes)

stapes (STAY peez) — the smallest bone in the ear of all mammals

INDEX

031.02
A

Armentrout

The smallest

031.02
A

Armentrout

The smallest

DATE DUE	BORROWER'S NAME	ROOM NUMBER